UNCOVERING THE PAST:
ANALYZING PRIMARY SOURCES

THE BATTLE OF THE ALAMO

LYNN PEPPAS

Crabtree Publishing Company
www.crabtreebooks.com

Author: Lynn Peppas

Editor-in-Chief: Lionel Bender

Editors: Simon Adams, Ellen Rodger

Proofreaders: Laura Booth,
Wendy Scavuzzo

Project coordinator: Petrice Custance

Design and photo research: Ben White

Production: Kim Richardson

**Production coordinator and
prepress technician:** Ken Wright

Print coordinator: Margaret Amy Salter

Consultant: Amie Wright,
The New York Public Library

**Produced for Crabtree Publishing
Company by Bender Richardson White**

Photographs and reproductions:
Bridgeman Images: front cover (James Edwin (1903-95) / Private Collection / © Look and Learn), Alamy: 6 (Everett Collection Historical), 20 (Reuters), 26 Btm (AF archive), 36 (World History Archive), 37 (Niday Picture Library), 38–39 (dbimages); Bridgeman Images: 24 (Private Collection, Peter Newark American Pictures); Getty Images: 28 (Library of Congress), 29 (Getty Images), 40 (Witold Skrypczak); Library of Congress: 3 (LC-USZC4-6127), 4, 6, 8 Top Left (Icon) (LC-DIG-highsm-28371), 8 Btm (LC-USZC4-6127), 10, 12, 14 Top Left (Icon) (LC-DIG-pga-04179), 12–13 (LC-USZ62-1273), 16, 18, 20 Top Left (Icon) (LC-DIG-highsm-27795), 18 (LC-DIG-highsm-27900), 22, 24, 26, 28, 30, 32 Top Left (Icon) (LC-USZC4-2133), 25 (LC-USZC4-2133), 26–27, 30–31 (LC-DIG-highsm-27907), 32 (LC-USZC4-6209), 33 (LC-DIG-highsm-27929), 34, 36 Top Left (Icon) (LC-USZC4-10045); Shutterstock: 1 (NeonLight), 14–15 (Philip Lange), 38, 40 Top Left (Icon) (Waehasman Waedarase), 41 (Salvador Aznar); Texas State Library and Archives Commission: 19 Btm (Bonham Collection); Topfoto: 4–5, 7, 8 Top Rt, 9 Btm, 15, 16–17, 19 top, 21, 22–23, 34–35 (The Granger Collection), 13 Btm (The Image Works), 10–11 (World History Archive), 19 Bottom Left (Courtesy of the Texas State Library and Archives Commission)
Map: Stefan Chabluk

Cover photo: Davy Crockett: Hero of the Alamo
Cover background: McConnell, James Edwin (1903-95) La Bastida Map, drawn for General Vicente Fisiloa of the Mexican Army in March 1836.
Title page photo: Historical re-enactment of the Battle of the Alamo

---

Library and Archives Canada Cataloguing in Publication

Peppas, Lynn, author
   The battle of the Alamo / Lynn Peppas.

(Uncovering the past : analyzing primary sources)
Includes bibliographical references and index.
Issued in print and electronic format.
ISBN 978-0-7787-3940-1 (hardcover).--
ISBN 978-0-7787-3944-9 (softcover).--
ISBN 978-1-4271-1999-5 (HTML)

   1. Alamo (San Antonio, Tex.)--Siege, 1836--Juvenile literature. 2. Texas--History--Revolution, 1835-1836--Juvenile literature. 3. Texas--History--To 1846--Juvenile literature.
4. United States--Politics and government--1945-1953--Juvenile literature. 5. United States--Politics and government--1953-1961--Juvenile literature. I. Title.

F390.P38 2017   j976.4'03   C2017-903631-9
                                       C2017-903632-7

Library of Congress Cataloging-in-Publication Data

Names: Peppas, Lynn, author.
Title: The Battle of the Alamo / Lynn Peppas.
Description: New York, New York : Crabtree Publishing Company, [2018] |
Series: Uncovering the past: analyzing primary sources | Includes bibliographical references and index. | Audience: Grades 4-6. | Audience: Ages 10-14.
Identifiers: LCCN 2017024375 (print) | LCCN 2017024623 (ebook) |
   ISBN 9781427119995 (Electronic HTML) |
   ISBN 9780778739401 (reinforced library binding) |
   ISBN 9780778739449 (pbk.)
Subjects: LCSH: Alamo (San Antonio, Tex.)--Siege, 1836--Juvenile literature.
Classification: LCC F390 (ebook) | LCC F390 .P38 2018 (print) |
   DDC 976.4/03--dc23
LC record available at https://lccn.loc.gov/2017024375

Crabtree Publishing Company
www.crabtreebooks.com   1-800-387-7650

Printed in Canada/082017/EF20170629

Copyright © 2018 CRABTREE PUBLISHING COMPANY. All rights reserved. No part of this publication may be reproduced, stored in a retrieval system or be transmitted in any form or by any means, electronic, mechanical, photocopying, recording, or otherwise, without the prior written permission of Crabtree Publishing Company. In Canada: We acknowledge the financial support of the Government of Canada through the Canada Book Fund for our publishing activities.

Published in Canada
Crabtree Publishing
616 Welland Ave.
St. Catharines, ON
L2M 5V6

Published in the United States
Crabtree Publishing
PMB 59051
350 Fifth Avenue, 59th Floor
New York, NY 10118

Published in the United Kingdom
Crabtree Publishing
Maritime House
Basin Road North, Hove
BN41 1WR

Published in Australia
Crabtree Publishing
3 Charles Street
Coburg North
VIC, 3058

UNCOVERING THE PAST

INTRODUCTION: THE PAST COMES ALIVE 4
    The importance of history and how it has shaped our lives today; an introduction to the Battle of the Alamo.

HISTORICAL SOURCES: TYPES OF EVIDENCE 10
    The two main types of historical evidence—primary sources and secondary sources—and how to distinguish them.

ANALYZING EVIDENCE: INTERPRETATION 16
    The importance of interpreting sources and their context; how to interpret bias; the problems of foreign languages and translations.

THE STORY UNCOVERED: BATTLE OF THE ALAMO 22
    The outbreak of the Texan Revolution; the Siege of Béxar and the Battle of the Alamo; the myth of Davy Crockett; the final battle at San Jacinto.

DIFFERENT VIEWS: AFTER THE BATTLE 34
    Texas, from independent republic to American state; the war of 1846–1848 between the United States and Mexico.

MODERN EXAMPLES: HISTORY REPEATED 38
    Revolution in Ukraine in 2014 as a modern equivalent of the Battle of the Alamo story; relations between Mexico and the United States today.

Timeline 42
Bibliography 44
Internet Guidelines 45
Glossary 46
Index 48

INTRODUCTION

THE PAST COMES ALIVE

*"I am besieged [surrounded], by a thousand or more of the Mexicans under Santa Anna — I have sustained a continual **bombardment** & **cannonade** for 24 hours & have not lost a man — . . . I shall never surrender or retreat . . ."*

Letter written by Lieutenant-Colonel William B. Travis from the Alamo "To the people of Texas & All Americans in the World," February 24, 1836

The Battle of the Alamo is a **legendary** story that has been retold in books, songs, and movies. In February 1836, hundreds of Texan soldiers at the Alamo in San Antonio, Texas, fought off thousands of Mexican soldiers for days during the Texas Revolution. At the final battle, all the Texan soldiers lost their lives. Yet these people live on in memory as some of the bravest heroes in American **history**.

Have you ever wondered how we know the story of the Alamo, especially when no Texan soldiers survived the battle? What has survived from that event—and can tell the story even today—is a collection of documents, records, and **artifacts**. These pieces of evidence are called **primary sources**.

Historians are people who gather and study primary sources from the past. They work in much the same way that detectives do to find clues about what really happened. You, too, can become a history detective by studying the clues that have been saved from the Battle of the Alamo to find out the true story of that conflict.

History repeats itself, which means that similar situations and problems occur time and time again. By studying history, we learn what has and has not worked in the past, and how events shape **society**. With this knowledge, we can understand how to deal with similar events or prevent them from ever happening again.

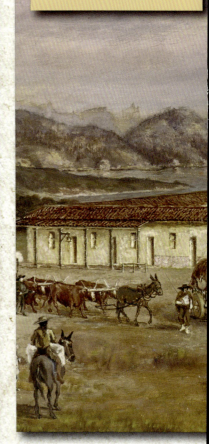

▼ Spain colonized and built **missions** throughout the Americas during the 1700s. One of these missions is shown here in this painting by Oriana Day called *A View of Mission San Carlos Borromeo de Carmelo*, in Carmel, California. **Roman Catholic** priests ran missions to **convert Indigenous** peoples to the religion.

4 UNCOVERING THE PAST

DEFINITIONS

Historians use special words to talk about time:

Decade: A period of 10 years,
Century: A period of 100 years,
Millennium: A period of 1,000 years.
Generation: Refers to a group of people who were born about the same time.

Era: A period of time dominated by an important characteristic, event, or person, for example, the colonial era.
Age: A long period of time dominated by an important event such as the Age of Exploration and Discovery.
History: The story of events in the past.

PERSPECTIVES

The American artist Oriana Day painted the Carmel Mission in 1834. What religious symbols are on top of of the highest buildings? Who do you think are the Spanish soldiers, and who are the Indigenous peoples in this painting? How are they different from each other? What do you think the story is behind this scene?

BATTLE OF THE ALAMO 5

INTRODUCTION

THE STORY OF THE ALAMO

Spanish explorers arrived in what is now known as Mexico in the early 1500s. Soon afterward, they took possession of the land and control of the Indigenous peoples living there. They explored northward and claimed areas that are now known as Florida, New Mexico, California, Arizona, and Texas. In the 1700s, they built numerous missions throughout the region. These were run by priests who worked to convert the indigenous populations to **Catholicism** and Spanish **culture**, and **colonize** the **frontier**. In 1744, the Spaniards built a mission at San Antonio, Texas, that later became known as the Alamo.

The Alamo was protected with an outer wall because of the ongoing conflicts between the Spanish and some Native American nations such as the Comanches and Apaches. In

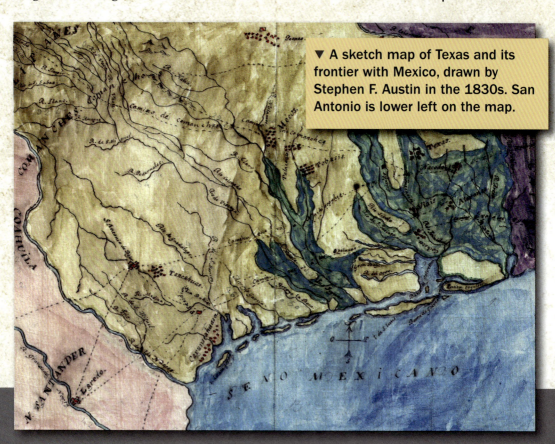

▼ A sketch map of Texas and its frontier with Mexico, drawn by Stephen F. Austin in the 1830s. San Antonio is lower left on the map.

"... I have labored **diligently** and faithfully and with pure intentions to cover the Wilderness of Texas with an Agricultural and [useful] population and to make it a State of the Mexican **Republic**..."

Stephen F. Austin writing to George Fisher, January 15, 1834 the late 1700s, the Spaniards turned the Alamo into a military **outpost** to protect the area from possible invasions by the French, Indigenous peoples, or Americans. The Alamo was **strategically** important because it was situated on a well-known trail into the heart of Texas.

PERSPECTIVES

Do you think the Texian cowboy in the foreground looks like a typical cowboy? How is he dressed differently? Are his actions the same as a modern cowboy's?

DEFINITIONS

Terms, names of groups of people, and names of places often change over a period of time. The words listed below will help you understand the proper **context** of primary sources that have been used in this book.

Anglo: A term for people whose native culture is English, and who speak the English language.

Béxar: The name of the area now known as San Antonio, Texas.

Empresario: A Spanish-language term used for a person in a leadership role over a group.

Negro: An offensive term used historically for people of African or African-American descent. In the past—more than 50 years ago—it was an acceptable term but is considered rude and offensive today.

Spaniard: A person born in Spain.

Tejano: A person who lived in Texas but whose native culture was Mexican.

Texian: A person who lived in Texas but whose native culture was English or American. *Texian* is the historical term used by colonists in the 1800s. The modern term is *Texan*.

▼ This line **engraving**, entitled *Vaqueros, 1839*, was based on a **lithograph** created in 1839. *Vaqueros* is a Spanish term for a cowboy.

BATTLE OF THE ALAMO 7

INTRODUCTION

THE UNITED STATES AND MEXICO

In the early 1800s, Americans wanted to expand their territories to the north, south, and west of the original 13 states. The War of 1812—a conflict between the Americans and British who had settled in Upper and Lower Canada—was an unsuccessful attempt by Americans to gain land to the north.

In 1810, Indigenous peoples in Mexico fought for their freedom from Spanish rule during the Mexican **Revolution.** Mexico won its **independence** from Spain in 1821. The Mexican government wanted to populate the wild frontier of Texas. They invited Americans to move to Texas under the conditions that they **revoke** their American citizenship, pledge **allegiance** to Mexico, and convert to Catholicism. New colonies in Texas

▲ Stephen Fuller Austin (1793–1836) was the first empresario of Texas. He brought hundreds of American families to settle along the Brazos River in 1821.

◀ This room is inside the Spanish governor's palace in San Antonio, Texas. The palace was built in 1749 and served as the office for the captain of the presidio, a Spanish term for a fort.

"I must say as to what I have seen of Texas it is the garden spot of the world. The best land and the best **prospects** for health I ever saw, and I do believe it is a fortune to any man to come here. There is a world of country here to settle . . ."

David (Davy) Crockett, writing to his children about Texas, January 9, 1836

were organized by Anglo political leaders called empresarios. The first empresario to enter Texas was Stephen F. Austin, who settled about 300 American families along the Brazos River in December 1821.

In the 1830s, the Mexican government worried that the United States would expand into its territories. They introduced the Law of April 6, 1830, which did not allow any new Anglos to **immigrate** to Texas. Mexican military sites were established to stop illegal immigration. The Mexican government also threatened to abolish, or put an end to, slavery but instead agreed that no new slaves could be brought to Texas and any children born to slaves were automatically freed.

The Texians did not like these, and other, changes. Texians and Tejanos gathered at **conventions** in 1832 and 1833 and wrote their own **constitution**. The Mexican government refused to change their laws which fueled the Texas Revolution in October 1835. The Battle of the Alamo was the most famous battle of the Texas Revolution. The Alamo was protected by less than 200 Texan soldiers. Mexican president and general Antonio López de Santa Anna arrived with an army of more than 1,000 soldiers on February 23, 1836. Even though they were greatly outnumbered, the Texian soldiers held the Mexican army off until March 6 when all the Texian soldiers were killed. Over time, the Battle of the Alamo became a symbol of bravery for the Texas Revolution, and later on, for American **patriotism**.

▼ This photograph is of a letter written by Stephen F. Austin to Andrew Jackson Donelson in 1836. In it, Austin suggests the United States consider **annexing** Texas.

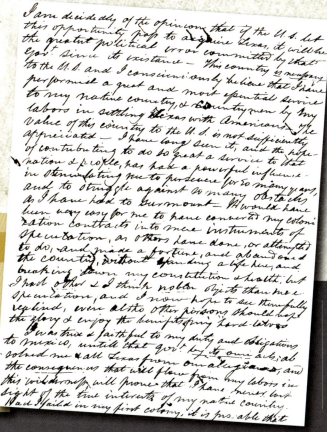

EVIDENCE RECORD CARD

Letter to U.S. **diplomat**
LEVEL Primary source
MATERIAL Handwritten letter
LOCATION Texas
DATE 1836
SOURCE Cornell University Library Collections

BATTLE OF THE ALAMO 9

HISTORICAL SOURCES

TYPES OF EVIDENCE

"General [Vicente] Guerrero came to the office of the presidency of the republic. . . . Among the first acts of his administration, was one to free all the negroes . . ."

Telegraph and Texas Register, January 23, 1836; General Guerrero was a Mexican military leader

Have you ever found a photograph or an old toy that brings back a memory from your past? Both are sources of information that tell about you, and are part of your history. If you post on Facebook, keep a diary or journal, or save a keepsake from your past, you've recorded a source of information called a primary source. If a historian in the year 3018 were to study the sources you'd created, they would be able to tell what young people were like in the early 2000s.

Historians learn about the past by gathering and investigating sources called primary sources. A primary source is a piece of information that was used, created, or recorded firsthand from a particular time or event in the past. Sometimes, interviews with people who witnessed an event are recorded days, weeks, or even years afterward. But the source of information is from their personal recollection or memory of the event and is considered a primary source.

Primary sources are preserved, or kept, and handed down through time so that we never forget the past. They are saved in places such as public libraries and museums. Some online **archives** take photographs of all types of primary sources and create databases that you can search and study.

▶ This movie poster advertises the 1960 historical epic film, *The Alamo,* which John Wayne produced, directed, and starred in. It reenacted the 1836 Battle of the Alamo.

ANALYZE THIS

Hollywood movies such as *The Alamo* are often not entirely historically correct. Considering that this film was made by Americans for an American audience, how might it be **biased** (see page 20)? What clues shape your opinion?

BATTLE OF THE ALAMO 11

HISTORICAL SOURCES

PRIMARY SOURCES
The Battle of the Alamo happened almost 200 years ago and some sources of information from that time have been lost or destroyed. Photographs were extremely rare in the early 1800s and photographic evidence from the Battle of the Alamo does not exist. At that time, people wrote journals, or letters that were delivered by carriers on horses. Artifacts such as parts of the Alamo as well as guns, cannons, and knives used during the battle have been preserved. Newspapers, official documents, and artworks have also been kept that are telling pieces of evidence of what happened during the Texas Revolution and the Battle of the Alamo.

A primary source is directly related to the topic you're researching. It represents firsthand knowledge of the topic because it was created by someone who participated in or witnessed the topic or event.

Examples of primary sources include:
- The diary of someone who experienced the topic or event you're researching
- Photographs taken at the location and time of the event
- Interview with someone who experienced the event
- Map of the location and its surroundings
- Newspaper articles of contemporary events or topics
- Documents or letters created at the time
- Physical objects from the location and time

SECONDARY SOURCES
An additional layer of information about an event comes from **secondary sources**. A secondary source is a description or interpretation of an era or event made

▲ This political cartoon by American artist Henry R. Robinson was published in 1836. Sam Houston (left) is saying to Santa Anna and Cos (center and right): "You are two bloody villains, and to treat you as you deserve, I ought to have you shot as an example! Remember the Alamo and Fannin!" (See page 30 for the story of James Fannin.)

". . . that conflict of arms was bloody, because the chief Travis, who commanded the forces of the Alamo, would not enter into any **capitulation**, and his responses were insulting. . . . the **obstinacy** of Travis and his soldiers was the cause of the death of the whole of them, for not one would surrender."

Santa Anna writing to Henry McArdle, March 16, 1874

by a person who did not experience it firsthand. It is created after an era or event has occurred. Secondary sources have used one or more primary sources to form opinions or reach conclusions. They have collected evidence and interpreted it for you already. Much of the history of the Battle of the Alamo is based on secondary sources. These, too, are archived.

Examples of secondary sources include:
- Encyclopedias and textbooks
- Newspaper and magazine articles that provide commentary or opinion
- Maps created today to show historical information
- Interview of an expert on a topic
- Documentaries
- Reconstruction illustrations and models
- Movies
- Websites
- Museum displays (that may include primary sources)

ANALYZE THIS

What types of things do you think an **archaeologist** might find at the Alamo? Do you recognize any of the tools they are using? How can finding artifacts from 1836 help people learn about what happened at the Alamo?

◀ Texas archaeologists and students found artifacts from the Texas Revolution along the north wall of the Alamo long barracks in 2006.

HISTORICAL SOURCES

DISTINGUISHING SOURCES

One way to determine if a document or an artifact is a primary or secondary source is to ask yourself: "Did the person who created this source of information participate in, or witness, the event or era?" If the answer is yes, then it's a primary source. If the answer is no, then it's a secondary source.

For example, take a look at the quote on page 4, given by Texian soldier William Travis present at the Alamo. This quote from his handwritten letter proves that Travis participated in the Battle of the Alamo. It is a primary source. But the song lyric quoted below from "Remember the Alamo" was written by Jane Bowers, who was born in 1921. Bowers couldn't have possibly been at the Alamo in the 1800s and even though this song "remembers" the Alamo, it is a secondary source.

But take care: Not all stories that feature the Battle of the Alamo are entirely true. Just because a book or movie is based on a historical event, it doesn't mean that everything in the story actually occurred. Often in historical drama or fiction, writers add or **embellish** characters, actions, and conversations that never really happened. Secondary sources such as encyclopedias and textbooks provide more reliable information.

If you are writing a report or summary of a historical event, try to get as many primary sources as you can. Sometimes these are difficult or costly to get, so you must rely on secondary sources. Choose a variety of sources where possible. Some sources may be good for visual evidence, others for written material. Beware, the quality of sources can vary—see the next chapter.

PERSPECTIVES

What are the structural similarities between these two images of the Alamo? What are the differences? Which image do you think resembles the Alamo more accurately at the time of the Battle of the Alamo? Why?

"Hey Santa Anna, we're killing your soldiers below!
That men, wherever they go will remember the Alamo"

"Remember the Alamo," written by Jane Bowers, around 1955, and since performed by musicians including Johnny Cash, Donovan, and Willie Nelson

14 UNCOVERING THE PAST

▲ An American wood engraving of the Alamo from 1854 shows the effect that the Battle of the Alamo had on the building.

◀ The Alamo was first called the Mission San Antonio de Valero. Spanish soldiers who came from the town Alamo de Parras nicknamed it the Alamo. *Alamo* is the Spanish word for the cottonwood tree.

EVIDENCE RECORD CARD

Modern photograph of tourists walking outside of the Alamo

LEVEL Secondary source
MATERIAL Photograph
LOCATION San Antonio, Texas
DATE April 11, 2016
SOURCE Shutterstock

ANALYZING EVIDENCE

INTERPRETATION

"Permit me, through you to volunteer my services in the present struggle of Texas without conditions. I shall receive nothing, either in the form of service pay, or lands, or rations."
— James Butler Bonham writing to Sam Houston, December 1, 1835

Historians figure out what happened during a past event by gathering and studying numerous primary sources. Each source provides a different piece of the puzzle. All primary sources are created for a specific reason. Historians analyze a source by asking what kind of a source it is and who was meant to see or use it. This is called sourcing. Sourcing gives you the context—the setting, conditions, time, and place. It also tells you how truthful or reliable a primary source may be. It is the process of asking the following questions:

- What is the primary source and why was it created?
- When and where was the source created?
- What else was happening around the same time?
- What does the source claim, say, show, or prove?
- Are there other primary sources that agree with or oppose what this source is saying/claiming/proving/showing?
- Why might this be?

For example, sourcing the quote at the top of this page tells us it is from a letter that James Butler Bonham wrote in 1835 to Texan major-general Sam Houston (see page 19). It lets Houston know that Bonham was "volunteering his services." One would expect his services included joining Houston's Texan army. The date the letter was written tells us that it was written during the Texas Revolution, and that Bonham eagerly supported the Texian cause.

UNCOVERING THE PAST

▼ Mexican forces laid siege to the Alamo for 13 days before initiating a full-out battle on March 6, 1836.

PERSPECTIVES

This engraving is entitled *Texas: The Alamo, 1836*. What do you think the large building in the background is called? What type of weapons are the soldiers using? What is at the end of their weapons? What flag is in the center of this picture?

EVIDENCE RECORD CARD

Texas: The Alamo, 1836
LEVEL Secondary source
MATERIAL Engraving
LOCATION San Antonio, Texas
DATE Unknown
SOURCE The Granger Collection/Topfoto

BATTLE OF THE ALAMO **17**

ANALYZING EVIDENCE

INTERPRETING EVIDENCE

All information given in primary sources might not necessarily be correct. As a historian, you must carefully source information to determine why it was created. One way to determine the truth and reliability of a source is if you find more than one source that tells you the same information.

Context is important for the history of the Battle of the Alamo. During the 1830s, the U.S. government wanted the nation to expand to the Pacific Ocean. This was later referred to as their **Manifest Destiny**. Texas—to the west—was part of this national endeavor. It shaped the country's politics and military actions.

Context is important when considering the quote at the bottom of this page, taken from the broadside shown opposite. Clearly, the information is incorrect because we know today that no American defenders survived the Battle of the Alamo. We are sure of this because there are many sources that give the same information—that all American, Texian, and Tejano soldiers died during the Battle of the Alamo. Yet you see here that the creator of this source from March 1836 wants the reader to think the opposite is true. But even though this primary material obviously gives you incorrect

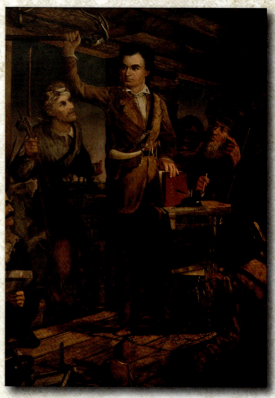

▲ The central figure in this painting is Stephen F. Austin. Austin was the first American empresario to move to Texas and start a **colony** with other Americans in 1821.

"... Gen. St. Anna arrived at that place with 2500 more men, and demanded a surrender of the fort held by 150 Texians ... but was repelled with the loss of 500 men, and the Americans lost none."

Text from the broadside shown opposite

PERSPECTIVES

This painting was done by Henry McArdle in 1875, long after the Battle of the Alamo. What does it tell you about the colonists? Do you think it is realistic? Why do you think the artist created it?

information, it also gives you an important insight into the objective of the piece. The creator wanted Americans to move to Texas by reassuring them that the Mexicans had lost the battle and that no American lives were lost.

So this "lie" actually gives evidence that Americans wanted to spread their territory into Texas and beyond.

▶ Broadsides, such as this one, were printed posters displayed in public places that spread news or announcements. They were meant to be seen for only a short time, then be thrown away. Luckily, this one survived and gives evidence of the past.

TEXAS FOREVER!!

The usurper of the South has failed in his efforts to enslave the freemen of Texas.

The wives and daughters of Texas will be saved from the brutality of Mexican soldiers.

Now is the time to emigrate to the Garden of America.

A free passage, and all found, is offered at New Orleans to all applicants. Every settler receives a location of

EIGHT HUNDRED ACRES OF LAND.

On the 23d of February, a force of 1000 Mexicans came in sight of San Antonio, and on the 25th Gen. St. Anna arrived at that place with 2500 more men, and demanded a surrender of the fort held by 150 Texians, and on the refusal, he attempted to storm the fort, twice, with his whole force, but was repelled with the loss of 500 men, and the Americans lost none. Many of his troops, the liberals of Zacatecas, are brought on to Texas in irons and are urged forward by the promise of the women and plunder of Texas.

The Texian forces were marching to relieve St. Antonio, March the 2d. The Government ____ is supplied with plenty of arms, ammunition, provisions, &c. &c.

ANALYZE THIS

What does the language and style of writing of Bonham's letter tell you about customs and traditions of the time? Today, would you consider a handwritten letter to be a better primary source than a typewritten letter, a tweet, or a blog?

◀ This letter written by James Butler Bonham to Sam Houston on December 1, 1835, is an important primary source.

BATTLE OF THE ALAMO 19

ANALYZING EVIDENCE

INTERPRETING BIAS

Sourcing also involves interpreting the **bias** with which almost every source of information—whether it is primary or secondary—is created. Bias is the personal outlook, prejudices, or opinions that every person has. Bias is not a bad thing: Everybody has some degree of bias when writing journals, letters, and artworks. Even you can have biased views that you have absorbed through TV, social media, your friends, and your teachers. But it is important to consider the bias in sources you look at so you can understand them better.

For example, consider the letter written by Texian Alamo commander William Travis (see page 4). Those reading the letter know that Travis supported the Texas Revolution and was fighting to break ties with Mexico. This would be his bias. On the other hand, a Mexican soldier would have an opposite bias and support Mexico's

▼ This handwritten report of the Battle of the Alamo was probably written by the Mexican colonel José Enrique de la Peña. Once believed to be a fake, it is a unique eyewitness account with a Mexican bias.

ANALYZE THIS

Can you read the words on de la Peña's manuscript? What language is it written in? Why is it important to learn about the event from evidence written by participants on different sides of the battle?

20 UNCOVERING THE PAST

claim to Texas. Both men had valid claims to what they believed in. But for sourcing purposes, when you read either source it is important to recognize that each was writing from his own personal bias or perspective (point of view).

Bias is also found in secondary sources. A textbook written for American students may focus on different perspectives and opinions than a textbook written for Mexican students. Again, you must interpret the bias in almost all sources to get to the bottom of what happened.

LANGUAGE AND TRANSLATIONS

Sometimes, sources are written in a language that is foreign to you. For the Battle of the Alamo, Mexican- or Tejano-created sources were often recorded in Spanish. If you cannot read Spanish, you must read a translated version of the same document. This means that a **translator** who is **fluent** in both Spanish and English has read a Spanish source and has rewritten it in English. Sometimes, the words of one language cannot be replaced precisely in another language and the meaning is changed slightly. A translation may not have the exact meaning that the original creator had intended it to have.

> **PERSPECTIVES**
>
> Who are the forces shown here in blue? What are they trying to do? Does it look as though they are succeeding? Whose flag is flying from the top of the Alamo?

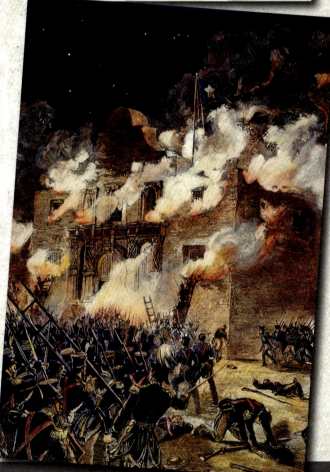

"TEXIANS! render every possible assistance, and soon shall you enjoy your liberty [freedom] and your property, which is the wish of your country man and friend, John N. Seguin, June 21, 1836."
Juan N. Seguín, *Telegraph and Texas Register*, September 21, 1836

▲ Mexican forces lay siege to the Alamo in this color engraving created in the 1800s.

BATTLE OF THE ALAMO **21**

THE STORY UNCOVERED

BATTLE OF THE ALAMO

*"How Travis and his hundred fell,
Amid a thousand foemen slain!
They died the Spartan's death,
But not in hopeless strife—
Like brothers died, and their expiring breath
Was Freedom's breath of life!"*

From "Hymn of the Alamo" by Reuben M. Potter, written October 1836

The Texas Revolution started in September 1835 when Mexican ruler Santa Anna sent a military force to take back a cannon it had loaned to the residents of Gonzales, Texas, for protection. The colonists were upset with the Mexican government and refused to give it back. Fighting broke out between the rebellious Texians and Tejanos and the Mexican military force. This became the Battle of Gonzales. The Mexican force retreated without the cannon, and the Texian and Tejano colonists claimed their first victory. But they knew the Mexican forces would be back. So they organized a revolutionary army made up of Texian and Tejano citizens and elected Stephen F. Austin as their commander.

In October, the revolutionary army laid **siege** to a Mexican force in San Antonio, home of the Alamo. This was known as the Siege of Béxar (San Antonio). After a few skirmishes were fought, Mexican forces, under Mexican general Cos, surrendered the Alamo on December 9, 1835 and returned to Mexico.

▶ In this painting—a secondary source—Texian leader William B. Travis is shown gathering his soldiers during the Siege of the Alamo, 1836.

22 UNCOVERING THE PAST

PERSPECTIVES

Which of these men depicted here is William B. Travis? Why do you think this? Do you think this is a good representation of the weapons, clothing, and hairstyles for the 1830s? How might you prove or disprove this?

BATTLE OF THE ALAMO 23

THE STORY UNCOVERED

SIEGE OF THE ALAMO

Many of the soldiers in the revolutionary army were simply farmers and citizens, not trained soldiers. Many returned to their families and homes after the skirmishes. They left the Alamo under the control of a much smaller force of about 150 soldiers and a few citizens because they thought the Mexicans would not return until late in the spring.

However, on February 23, the Mexican army under the command of Santa Anna surprised those at the Alamo and arrived with an army of more than 1,000 soldiers. Santa Anna sent one of his colonels to negotiate an unconditional surrender with the Texians, but their leader William Travis refused. The Mexicans laid siege to the Alamo.

On February 24, James Bowie, who shared command with Travis, became very ill. Travis wrote his famous letter "To the people of Texas & All Americans in the World." The letter was a plea for more reinforcements. It was carried by Texian soldier and messenger Albert Martin to an officer in Gonzales, Texas. In fact, a number of letters asking for

▼ This is a copy of the *La Bastida Map* that was drawn for Mexican army general Vicente Filisola in March 1836. The map shows the town, then called Béxar (Bejar), and the Alamo.

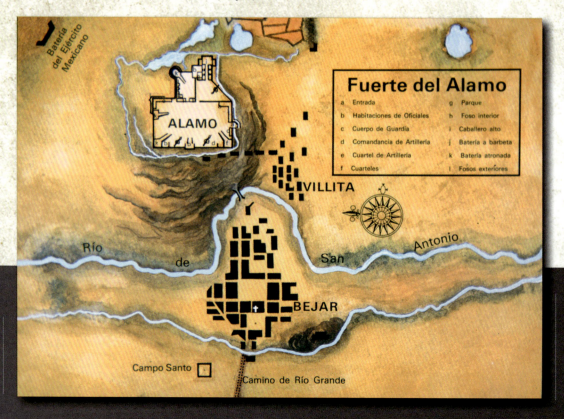

help were sent out by messengers such as Tejano Juan Seguín, and American soldier James Bonham. These letters have been preserved and remain as important primary sources for the Battle of the Alamo today.

> **PERSPECTIVES**
>
> How can you tell which fighters are the Texians and which are the Mexicans? Do you think the image is a realistic or romantic idea of the battle? Which side is the woman on? What nationality do you think the artist, Percy Morgan, is: Anglo or Mexican? Why do you think this?

▼ After a 13-day siege, Mexican forces launched an attack on the Texian forces at the Alamo.

"... This attack was extremely injudicious [unwise] and in opposition to military rules, for our own men were exposed not only to the fire of the enemy but also to that of our own columns attacking the other Fronts; and our soldiers being formed in close columns, all shots that were aimed too low, struck the backs of our foremost men..."

Mexican general Vicente Filisola in 1849, remembering the Battle of the Alamo

THE STORY UNCOVERED

THE BATTLE OF THE ALAMO

Some soldiers came to the aid of the Alamo defenders, including Texian, American, and Tejano fighters. Thirty-two soldiers arrived at the Alamo from Gonzales, Texas, on March 1. Promises of hundreds more troops came in, but those soldiers did not arrive in time.

Meanwhile, on March 2, during a meeting at Washington-on-the-Brazos, a group of Texians voted for independence from Mexico. The Texas Declaration of Independence was mostly written by George Childress, who had illegally immigrated to Texas in December 1835. The Republic of Texas was born. On March 4, politician and newcomer to Texas, Sam Houston, was elected as major-general of the republic's army.

Back at the Alamo, the siege lasted for 13 days. During that time, the Alamo

PERSPECTIVES

Who appears to be winning the Battle of the Alamo in this painting? How does the artist's bias show in this work? If a Mexican artist painted the same scene in 1905, how might his or her work differ from McArdle's?

PERSPECTIVES

How realistic do you think this movie set of the Alamo really is? What might have looked different during the actual battle in 1836?

▼ This photograph is of the movie set of *The Alamo*, released in 2004. It was not filmed at the Alamo but rather the set was created and filmed in Texas.

26

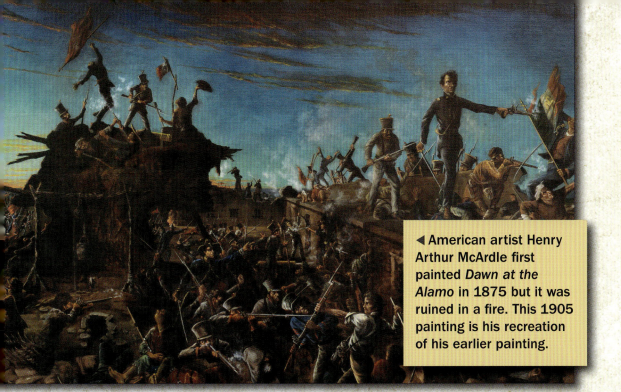

◀ American artist Henry Arthur McArdle first painted *Dawn at the Alamo* in 1875 but it was ruined in a fire. This 1905 painting is his recreation of his earlier painting.

defenders fired on the Mexican troops as they dug trenches, built **batteries**, and fired ammunition at the Alamo's walls. But they were running low of ammunition, water, and food. At midnight on March 6, the Mexican forces got into position for an assault and attacked at about 5:30 A.M. The Alamo's defenders put up a brave fight. Mexican colonel José Enrique de la Peña wrote that a shot from the defenders' cannon wiped out almost half of one Mexican company. Alamo commander William B. Travis was one of the first soldiers to die from a gunshot to the head. But within 90 minutes of combat, the defenders had been defeated.

Even though no Texian soldiers survived the Battle of the Alamo, a few citizens living with the defenders did. A number of slaves were reported as having survived. Susannah Dickinson and her 15-month-old daughter Angelina survived the battle, too. She was the wife of Texian defender Almaron Dickinson. The slaves and Susannah later gave their story of what happened at the battle. Their stories have been preserved and are important primary sources that give an American perspective of what happened.

"On the north battery of the fortress lay the lifeless body of Colonel Travis on the gun carriage shot only in the forehead. Toward the west in a small fort opposite the city we found the body of Colonel Crockett. Colonel Bowie was found dead in his bed in one of the rooms on the south side."

Eyewitness report from Francisco Antonio Ruiz on the aftermath of the Battle of the Alamo, published in the *San Antonio Light*, March 6, 1907

THE STORY UNCOVERED

DAVY CROCKETT: MAN AND MYTH

The names of the Anglos involved in the Battle of the Alamo live on in legend as brave patriots who made the ultimate sacrifice for what they believed in. William Travis, James Bowie, and James Bonham are a few of these. Very little is known of the Tejano Texian soldiers, such as Gregorio Esparza, or 17-year-old Carlos Espalier, who also died and were considered heroes for the cause. But by far the most famous soldier present at the Alamo was legendary American frontiersman Davy Crockett.

PERSPECTIVES

The American soldier near the center of this painting is Davy Crockett. Can you tell which one he is? What item of clothing is Crockett wearing that he is famous for? How does this image of Crockett fit in with his legend and myths written about him?

▼ This painting, entitled *Gallant Defence*, shows Texian soldiers defending the Alamo against Mexican troops.

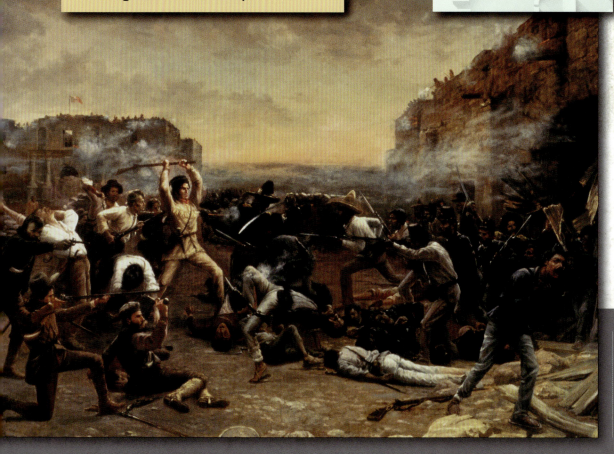

Crockett's adventures were well-known in the United States years before he arrived at the Alamo. He was a professional hunter and folk hero from Tennessee. He fought for the United States against the Creek Confederacy of Native Americans in the Creek War of 1813–1814. Crockett was also elected and served in Congress. He went west to Texas in November 1835 to explore the possibility of moving there with his family. Arriving in San Antonio de Béxar in February 1836, he joined William B. Travis at the Alamo. During the battle, survivors such as Susannah Dickinson reported to have seen Crockett killed early on. Travis's slave Joe also said he saw Crockett's dead body, surrounded by fallen Mexican soldiers.

Mexican soldiers said that five or six survivors were captured and taken to Santa Anna, then executed. Some of these accounts say that Davy Crockett was one of these men. Years later, the diary of Mexican lieutenant José Enrique de la Peña presented this version of the story, stating that Crockett and others surrendered and were then executed by Mexicans.

Historians compare, interpret, and analyze multiple primary source accounts to try to find the truth of what happened at the Alamo. Crockett's fame was known to Mexicans. But would the Mexican soldiers have recognized Crockett or did it make for a more exciting story if one of the prisoners was the famous American? Did Dickinson and Joe really see Crockett's dead body in the confusion and aftermath of the battle? We know that Crockett did not survive the Alamo. But we may never know for sure if he died at the Alamo or was executed shortly after.

"The fall of the Alamo and the massacre of its garrison . . . have never been fully and correctly narrated, and wild exaggerations have taken their place in popular legend."
Captain R. M. Potter published his account in the *San Antonio Herald*, 1860

▲ Davy Crockett, Indian Fighter was a Walt Disney production that aired in the mid-1950s. The stories were somewhat **fictitious** and **mythologize** the legendary American hero.

BATTLE OF THE ALAMO 29

THE STORY UNCOVERED

DECLARATION OF INDEPENDENCE

The Texians considered the Alamo a terrible loss. But it energized the revolution, as did a battle and a shocking massacre that followed less than a month later. Events were moving fast. The Texas Declaration of Independence was signed around the same time as the Alamo battle, officially setting up the Republic of Texas. Santa Anna's Mexican army was determined to crush the uprising.

MASSACRE AT GOLIAD

The Texians had seized Fort Defiance in Goliad at the beginning of the revolution. Now, knowing a Mexican force of 1,400 soldiers was on its way, Texan Commander-in-Chief Sam Houston ordered the 400 men in Goliad to retreat. But the Goliad commander, James Fannin, left it too late. On March 19, 1836, the retreating Texians met the advancing Mexican forces at Coleto Creek. The battle was brief and the Texans surrendered, believing they would be treated as prisoners of war. Instead, Santa Anna ordered them to be executed. More than 340 Texan soldiers were killed in what became known as the Goliad Massacre.

BATTLE OF SAN JACINTO

After the Alamo and the Battle of Coleto, it seemed that the Mexican forces under Santa Anna were unbeatable. Some colonists and soldiers packed up and fled to the United States. Most Texian soldiers were determined to continue the struggle for independence.

"Arriving at the other bank of the river, I looked around once more to where my comrades were dying, while the bullets of the still firing enemies whistled about me. The hellish exaltations [extreme happiness] of the enemy mixed with the cries of pain of my dying brothers sounded over to me."

Herman Ehrenberg, who escaped execution at Goliad, from his published memoir, *Texas And Its Revolution*, 1843

The final battle against the Mexicans was launched by Houston on April 21, 1836, at San Jacinto. Houston ordered the surprise attack at mid-afternoon when many of the Mexican soldiers were enjoying a siesta, their midday rest. The battle lasted about 20 minutes, in which time the Mexicans were defeated. Santa Anna managed to escape but was later captured. Bargaining for his freedom, he signed the Treaty of Valesco that recognized Texas's independence from Mexico. The Mexican government refused to honor the treaty. An uneasy relationship continued between Mexico and the Republic of Texas for years.

▼ This painting of 1895, *The Battle of San Jacinto*, shows Texian soldiers defeating Mexican troops.

EVIDENCE RECORD CARD

The Battle of San Jacinto
LEVEL Secondary source
MATERIAL Painting
CREATOR Henry Arthur McArdle
LOCATION San Jacinto, Texas
DATE 1895
SOURCE Library of Congress/State Capitol, Austin, Texas

PERSPECTIVES

Look at the uniforms and equipment of the two armies. What do you think it would be like to fight in such a battle? What shows how easy it was for the Texians to win the battle so quickly?

THE STORY UNCOVERED

TEXAS: FROM REPUBLIC TO AMERICAN STATE

The Republic of Texas held an election for president and a congress. Sam Houston, former commander-in-chief of the Texas army ran for president against Stephen F. Austin (see pages 8–9, 18). Austin was an empresario who brought 300 families from the United States to colonize Texas in 1821. Houston won and became the first elected president of Texas.

Most Texans wanted to be part of the United States. At that time, the United States decided not to **annex** Texas because it did not want to go to war with Mexico. Both countries had recently signed a trade agreement and the United States did not want to upset its neighbor. Also, Texas supported slavery. By annexing Texas, there would be more slave states than free states in the United States. Free states worried they would be made to accept slavery again. Eventually, Texas and the United States negotiated a Treaty of Annexation in 1844.

MEXICAN–AMERICAN WAR 1846–1848

The Mexican government officially regarded Texas as a state of Mexico. There was much unrest between the

▼ The American army clashed with Mexican forces under the command of General Santa Anna in April 1847 at the Battle of Cerro Gordo. Cerro Gordo was an important, strategic mountain pass that led to Mexico City.

PERSPECTIVES

This lithograph, entitled *The Flight of Santa Anna at the Battle of Cerro Gordo*, was created in about 1847. Why is Santa Anna dressed in red, green, and white? What do those colors represent? Compare the ground that the Americans are on to that of Santa Anna. Why is one side neat and cared for while the other is a wilderness? What does this show you about the bias of the lithographer Richard Magee?

32

two countries over the matter and on April 25, 1846 Mexican troops crossed the Rio Grande—considered by the Americans to be the Mexican–U.S. border. They attacked American troops stationed there. U.S. President James Polk retaliated and declared war against Mexico on May 13. The American forces invaded and occupied numerous Mexican states. In a final battle, they overtook Mexico's capital of Mexico City, at which time the Mexican government fled. Mexico signed the Treaty of Guadalupe Hidalgo on February 2, 1848.

The treaty officially recognized the annexation of Texas by the United States. At the same time, Mexico sold California, Utah, Nevada, and parts of Arizona, New Mexico, Colorado, and Wyoming to the United States for $15 million (equal to about $450 million today). The Mexican people were devastated at having lost great amounts of valuable land to the United States. The Americans felt it was their right to overtake the Mexican states because they had won the war. The outcome of the war created bad feelings and mistrust between the two countries that existed long after the war.

▼ **The Surrender of Santa Anna after the Battle of San Jacinto** (1836) was painted by American artist William Henry Huddle in 1886 to commemorate the 50th anniversary of the battle.

"The invasion of Texas by the Mexican forces… was threatened solely because Texas had determined, in accordance with a solemn resolution of the Congress of the United States, to annex herself to our Union, and under these circumstances it was plainly our duty to extend our protection over her citizens and soil."

U.S. President James Polk, May 11, 1846

DIFFERENT VIEWS

AFTER THE BATTLE

"Let us weep at the tomb of the brave Mexicans who died at the Alamo defending the honor and the rights of their country. They won lasting claim to fame and the country can never forget their heroic names."

Santa Anna, 1837

With the Treaty of Guadalupe Hidalgo in place, the United States gained much valuable land. But there were many people who were affected quite differently by the outcome, notably Mexicans, Tejanos, Native Americans, and enslaved African Americans. They were all involved in the history of this event and their perspectives are important to consider, too.

During the Texas Revolution and war, Mexico suffered the human loss of thousands of its young men killed and injured in the fighting. Because the United States attacked Mexico, many buildings, roads, and natural areas in Mexico were destroyed. It was a tremendous loss for Mexico to **cede** California, Utah, Nevada, and parts of Arizona, New Mexico, Colorado, and Wyoming. During **negotiations** of the treaty, Mexican commissioners strongly disagreed with almost all of the terms given and tried to change the outcome. In the end, they received only half of what they originally demanded. But having lost the war, there was little they could do to change things and they were forced to accept the terms the United States wanted.

Mexico resented being conquered and losing half its national lands to the United States. In Mexico, what the Americans referred to as the Mexican–American War was instead called the U.S. Intervention or the U.S. Invasion of Mexico. From just the different names given to the same event, you can see the points of view from an American or Mexican perspective.

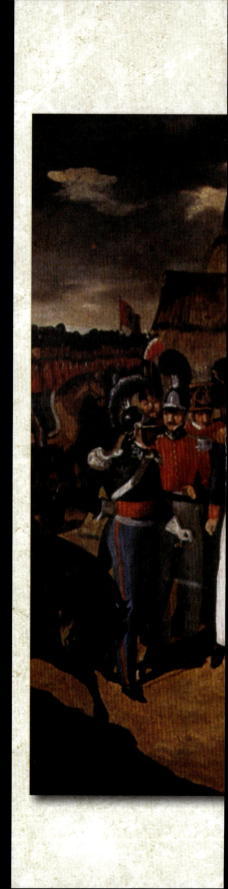

PERSPECTIVES

How is Santa Anna depicted in this painting by a Mexican artist? What do you think the artist would like you to think about Santa Anna when you view this painting? Now, look at other paintings with Santa Anna in them done by American artists. What is different in the American artists' paintings?

◀ Santa Anna is shown here in the center of this painting of a 1829 battle between Mexican and Spanish forces. He is pointing to the man on the horse. American sources often depict the Mexican military and political leader as a cruel and sometimes foolish person, but many Mexicans believe his legacy is much more honorable.

BATTLE OF THE ALAMO 35

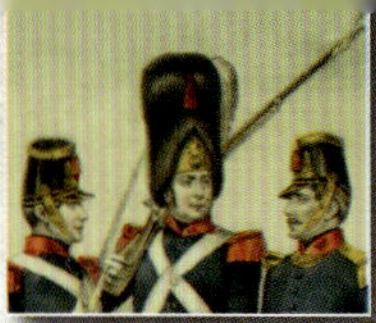

DIFFERENT VIEWS

FOREIGNERS IN THEIR HOMELAND

After the Treaty of Guadalupe Hidalgo, many Tejanos, Mexicans, and Native Americans living in the newly ceded areas suddenly found they were foreigners in their homeland. Tejano and Mexican families were often discriminated against because of their Mexican heritage. Some Tejanos and Mexicans living in the United States were not enfranchised, or allowed to vote, and could not hold political office. Even though they became American citizens, they were treated as **second-class citizens** and were not entitled to the same rights that other Americans enjoyed. Some Mexican families living in the newly ceded areas were suddenly homeless, with no income and no lands to call their own. They had few rights to fight against the U.S. government.

consent of the Senate thereof; and by the President of the Mexican Republic, with the previous approbation of its General Congress: and the ratifications shall be exchanged in the City of Washington in four months from the date of the signature hereof, or sooner if practicable.

In faith whereof, we, the respective Plenipotentiaries, have signed this Treaty of Peace, Friendship, Limits and Settlement, and have hereunto affixed our seals respectively. Done in Quintuplicate at the city of Guadalupe Hidalgo on the second day of February in the year of Our Lord one thousand eight hundred and forty-eight.

Presidente de los Estados Unidos de América con el consejo y consentimiento del Senado; y las ratificaciones se cangearán en la ciudad de Washington á los cuatro meses de la fecha de la firma del mismo Tratado, ó antes si fuere posible.

En fé de lo cual, nosotros los respectivos Plenipotenciarios hemos firmado y sellado por quintuplicado este tratado de Paz, Amistad, Límites y Arreglo definitivo, en la ciudad de Guadalupe Hidalgo el dia dos de Febrero del año de nuestro Señor mil ochocientos cuarenta y ocho.

N. P. Trist

Luis G. Cuevas

Bernardo Couto

Miguel Atristain

Bernardo Couto

Miguel Atristain

Luis G. Cuevas

N. P. Trist

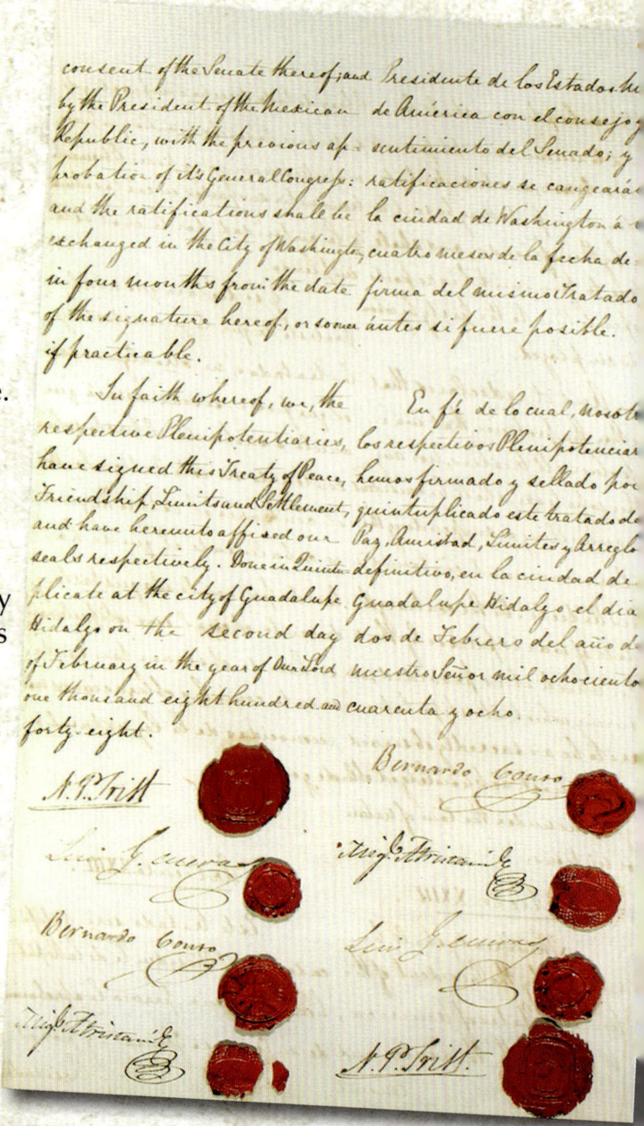

EVIDENCE RECORD CARD

The Treaty of Guadalupe Hidalgo
LEVEL Primary source
MATERIAL Document
LOCATION Mexico City, Mexico
DATE February 2, 1848
SOURCE Alamy Images

". . . The loss of Texas will inevitably [definitely] result in the loss of New Mexico and the Californias [for Mexico]. Little by little our territory will be absorbed, until only an insignificant [small and unimportant] part is left to us. . . ."

Mexico Secretary of War José María Tornel y Mendívil, 1837

▲ In the Treaty of Guadalupe Hidalgo, shown here, Mexico sold the United States more than half of its land. About 70,000 Mexicans living there became "foreigners" overnight.

> **PERSPECTIVES**
>
> What type of terrain are these soldiers located in? Do you think the soldiers shown here are American or Mexican? What type of vehicles are they using? What type of weapons are they using? Are they prepared for fierce warfare or skirmishes?

In the 1800s, the United States did not grant Native Americans citizenship of any type and they were not allowed to vote until the 1900s.

A small number of Americans, mostly from the north of the Mexican border, were also against the Mexican–American War. One reason was because they, like Mexico, were against slavery. Politically, allowing slavery in southern states could upset the balance between free and slave states and allow slavery throughout the United States. California voted to become a free state but, as in other newly acquired lands in the south, the slave trade grew in Texas as landowners began setting up large cotton and sugar plantations that required hundreds of slaves to operate.

Many Americans felt that westward expansion of the United States was justified, even though it cost many people their homelands and cultural identities. But thousands of others—some of them American citizens—held different points of view about the events that happened after the Battle of the Alamo.

▼ American forces raided Mexico in 1916 to capture Mexican revolutionary leader Pancho Villa. The military action almost brought war between the United States and Mexico again.

BATTLE OF THE ALAMO **37**

MODERN EXAMPLES

HISTORY REPEATED

"Slava Ukrayini! Heroyam Slava!"

A Ukrainian greeting and slogan, translated from Ukrainian reads: "Glory to Ukraine! Glory to the heroes!"

"History repeats itself," which means that over time, people experience similar situations to those that have happened in the past. Just as Texas revolted against the Mexican government in 1836 because many settlers disagreed with its laws, other countries have protested against their governments because they do not agree with their rulers. One of the many examples of modern revolts is the Ukrainian Revolution of 2014 known as Euromaidan.

In 2013, a majority of Ukrainian citizens wanted their president, Viktor Yanukovych, to sign an agreement to join the European Union (EU). The EU is an organization of 28 European countries with strong economic and political ties. But instead, Yanukovych signed an agreement with Russian president Vladimir Putin. Hundreds of thousands of Ukrainians united and protested against their government in the country's capital, Kiev. The Ukrainian government allowed a special riot police force called Berkut to use violence and weapons against protesters to end the conflict. In January and February 2014, thousands of Ukrainian protesters were injured or kidnapped, and more than 100 were killed by Berkut forces. Those who died during the conflict were called the Heavenly Hundred. Today, they are remembered as patriotic heroes who sacrificed their lives to defend their nation's rights, just as Alamo defenders did in 1836.

▶ The common border shared by Mexico and Texas is 1,254 miles (2,018 km) long. There are 25 international bridges and border crossings that allow visitors to travel between the United States and Mexico.

38 UNCOVERING THE PAST

ANALYZE THIS

This border crossing between Ciudad Juárez, Mexico, and El Paso, Texas, sees thousands of people crossing between the two countries every day. Notice the signs on top of the customs booths. One says "Cerrado" and the other says "Closed." What languages are these written in? Why are both languages needed?

BATTLE OF THE ALAMO 39

MODERN EXAMPLES

TEXAS SOVEREIGNTY

Most Texans recognize Texas as an American state, but some Texans have argued it is still a republic—a region that should be run by representatives of the people and not by federal government in Washington, D.C.

Before the U.S. Civil War (1861–1865), a majority of Texans voted to **secede** from the United States to join the Confederacy in March 1861. In 1869, in the Supreme Court case Texas v. White, it was ruled that the secession of Texas was illegal because states were not allowed to secede. A small minority of Texans still disagree with this ruling. The Republic of Texas and the Texas Nationalist Movement are two organizations that believe in the **sovereignty** of Texas. Both organizations work peacefully toward gaining independence for Texas from the United States so it can once again become a republic of its own.

U.S.–MEXICAN RELATIONS TODAY

Relations between the United States and Mexico since the Mexican–American War have, at times, been strained. In the Gadsden Purchase of 1853, the United States purchased from Mexico about 30,000 square miles (77,700 square km) of bordering lands known as the Mesilla Valley for $10 million to build a railroad. Mexico was in debt and felt threatened

ANALYZE THIS

Were the Heavenly Hundred heroes and the Alamo defenders both defending principles of democracy, human rights, or freedom, or all of these? Why is it important to remember their sacrifices? Should we honor them today?

"I regret and condemn the United States' decision to continue with the construction of a wall that, for years now, far from uniting us, divides us."

Mexican president Enrique Peña Nieto, *The New York Times*, January 26, 2017

▲ A noticeboard in the Ukraine commemorating the Heavenly Hundred heroes (see page 38).

that the United States would annex the territory anyway.

During the Mexican Revolution of 1910–1920, Mexican revolutionary leader Pancho Villa led an attack on the U.S. town of Columbus, New Mexico, on March 19, 1916. The revolutionary army killed 17 Americans and burned areas of the town. The United States retaliated by launching the Punitive Expedition of 1916–1917—a military raid in northern Mexico to capture Pancho Villa and his army, but it was unsuccessful. The Mexican government clashed with U.S. forces, feeling that the raid threatened Mexican sovereignty.

Mexican immigration to the United States has also been an area of tension between the two countries. Mexican laborers were invited to the United States to help build the railroads in 1882, and many more immigrated to the United States because of unrest during the Mexican Revolution in 1910. But in 1929, during the Great Depression, American workers strongly resented the Mexican-American and Mexican immigrant workforce. The U.S. government responded with forced, mass **deportations** of hundreds of thousands of Mexican-American citizens and legal Mexican immigrants. In 2005, the State of California passed the Apology Act for the 1930s Mexican Repatriation Program.

Today, hundreds of thousands of Mexicans illegally cross the border every year to relocate to the United States because they have no jobs, or make too little money at the jobs they do have. To try to control this, in 2016, incoming president Donald Trump proposed building a giant wall along the United States–Mexico border. Thus the legacy of the Battle of the Alamo continues.

PERSPECTIVES

How are the defenders of the Alamo portrayed in this monument? How do you think Mexicans and overseas visitors to the Alamo think of the battle when they see this and read the names of the fort's defenders?

▶ *The Spirit of Sacrifice* monument at San Antonio, Texas, completed in 1939, honors those Americans killed at the Battle of the Alamo.

BATTLE OF THE ALAMO **41**

TIMELINE

1500s Spanish explorers arrive in Central America and claim most of the lands today known as Mexico and the American states of Texas, New Mexico, Arizona, and California

1812–1814 United States declares war on British colonists in Upper and Lower Canada in an unsuccessful bid to annex lands

1830 Mexico passes law that restricts American immigration to Texas

September 1835 Battle of Gonzales begins the Texas Revolution

December 9, 1835 Mexican military surrenders the Alamo

February 24, 1836 Alamo commander William B. Travis writes his letter asking for reinforcements

March 7, 1836 Mexican forces attack the Alamo, killing of all the defenders

April 20, 1836 Sam Houston and the Texan army claim independence from Mexico

May 13, 1846 United States declares war on Mexico

September 1847 U.S. troops occupy Mexico City, ending the Mexican–American War

1800

1835

1852

1744 Spanish build a mission at Béxar de San Antonio (San Antonio) that is later known as the Alamo

1810 Mexicans revolt against Spanish rule

September 1821 Mexico wins independence from Spain

December 1821 Empresario Stephen Fuller Austin arrives in Texas with 300 American families

October 1835 Texas's revolutionary army lays siege to Béxar

February 23, 1836 Mexican army under Santa Anna lays siege to the Alamo

March 2, 1836 Texans vote for independence from Mexico and write the Texas Declaration of Independence

March 27, 1836 Goliad Massacre— James Fannin and about 341 Texan soldiers executed

April 25, 1846 Mexican troops cross the Rio Grande River and attack American troops on U.S. land

February 2, 1848 Treaty of Guadalupe Hidalgo is signed: Mexico recognizes U.S. annexation of Texas and sells southern lands to the United States for $15 million

42 UNCOVERING THE PAST

1853 Gadsden Purchase: Mexico sells the Mesilla Valley to the United States for $10 million

1861–1865 U.S. Civil War

1916–1917 U.S. troops raid Mexico to capture Mexican revolutionary leader Pancho Villa

2005 State of California passes Apology Act for the 1930s Mexican Repatriation Program

1853

2017

March 1861 Texas votes to secede from the United States and joins the Confederacy

1910 Mexican Revolution begins

1930 Mexican Repatriation Act deports hundreds of thousands of legal Mexican immigrants and Mexican-American citizens to Mexico during Great Depression

2016 Incoming U.S. President Donald Trump proposes the construction of a multibillion-dollar wall along the United States–Mexican border

Map of Texas at the time of the Battle of the Alamo

BATTLE OF THE ALAMO 43

BIBLIOGRAPHY

QUOTATIONS

p.4 William B. Travis letter: www.tsl.texas.gov/treasures/republic/alamo-01.html

p.6 Stephen F. Austin letter: www.tsl.texas.gov/treasures/giants/austin/austin-fisher-jan34-1.html

p.8 David Crockett letter: www.texianlegacy.com/crockettletter.html

p.10 Excerpt from an article published in the *Telegraph and Texas Register*, January 23, 1836: www.digitalhistory.uh.edu/disp_textbook.cfm?smtid=3&psid=3660

p.12 Santa Anna letter, March 16, 1874: www.tsl.texas.gov/treasures/republic/alamo/santa-anna-letter-01.html

p.14 Song lyrics from "Remember the Alamo," written by Jane Bowers, circa 1955: www.metrolyrics.com/remember-the-alamo-lyrics-johnny-cash.html

p.16 James Bonham letter: www.tsl.texas.gov/treasures/republic/alamo/bonham-letter.html

p.18 Text from broadside printed in 1836: Topfoto GR0110129_H

p.21 Juan N. Seguín, *Telegraph and Texas Register*, September 21, 1836: www.digitalhistory.uh.edu/disp_textbook.cfm?smtid=3&psid=3661

p.22 "Hymn of the Alamo" by Reuben M. Potter, written in October 1836: www.tsl.texas.gov/mcardle/alamo/alamo08.html

p.25 Vicente Filisola, firsthand account of the Battle of the Alamo, written up by Amelia Williams in *A Critical Study of the Siege of the Alamo and of the Personnel of Its Defenders*, Southwestern Historical Quarterly, July 1933: www.digitalhistory.uh.edu/disp_textbook.cfm?smtid=3&psid=3663

p.26 Francisco Antonio Ruiz, San Antonio Light, published March 6, 1907: www.tamu.edu/faculty/ccbn/dewitt/adp/archives/newsarch/ruizart.html

p.29 R. M. Potter, *Magazine of American History*, January 1878, Vol. II, No. 1: www.tamu.edu/faculty/ccbn/dewitt/adp/history/1836/accounts/potter/potter01.html

p.30 Herman Ehrenberg, *Texas And Its Revolution*, 1843: www.tamu.edu/faculty/ccbn/dewitt/goliadehrenberg.htm

p.33 James Polk, message on war with Mexico, May 11, 1846: www.pbs.org/weta/thewest/resources/archives/two/mexdec.htm

p.34 Santa Anna in *The Mexican Side of the Texas Revolution* by Carlos E. Castañeda, Dallas: 1928: www.digitalhistory.uh.edu/disp_textbook.cfm?smtid=3&psid=3662

p.36 José María Tornel y Mendívil, "Relations Between Texas, The United States of America and the Mexican Republic" Mexico, 1837: www.digitalhistory.uh.edu/disp_textbook.cfm?smtid=3&psid=3664

p.40 Enrique Peña Nieto, *The New York Times*, January 26, 2017: www.nytimes.com/2017/01/26/world/mexicos-president-cancels-meeting-with-trump-over-wall.html

TO FIND OUT MORE

Carey, Charles W., Jr. *The Mexican–American War.* New York: Enslow Publishing, 2017.

Doeden, Matt. *The Battle of the Alamo (Graphic History).* Mankato: Capstone Press, 2005.

Hale, Nathan. *Alamo All Stars (A Texas Tale).* New York: Amulet Books, 2016.

Nardo, Don. *The Alamo.* Detroit: Lucent Books/Gale Cengage Learning, 2013.

INTERNET GUIDELINES

Finding good source material on the Internet can sometimes be a challenge. When analyzing how reliable the information is, consider these points:

- Who is the author of the page? Is it an expert in the field or a person who experienced the event?
- Is the site well known and up to date? A page that has not been updated for several years probably has out-of-date information.
- Can you verify the facts with another site? Always double-check information.
- Have you checked all possible sites? Don't just look on the first page a search engine provides. Remember to try government sites and research papers.
- Have you recorded website addresses and names? Keep this data so you can backtrack and verify the information you want to use.

WEBSITES

The Alamo Museum
A website provides a chronology of events surrounding the Battle of the Alamo and short biographies of the defenders.
www.thealamo.org

Texas State Library and Archives Commission
A website with a digital collection of images, documents, and the history of Texas.
https://www.tsl.texas.gov/

Digital History
Provides the history of the Texas Revolution, Battle of the Alamo, and Mexican–American War through primary-source documents from all points of view.
http://www.digitalhistory.uh.edu

Texas State Historical Association
A website with historical narrative on the history of Texas with some primary-source documents included.
www.tshaonline.org/

PBS
Offers the history of Texas and some primary-source documents in "Archives of the West."
http://www.pbs.org/weta/thewest/resources/archives/

Project Gutenberg
Offers downloadable historical books such as Davy Crockett's autobiography, *A Narrative of the Life of Davy Crockett, of the State of Tennessee.*
www.gutenberg.org

GLOSSARY

allegiance Being true or devoted to someone, something, or a place

annex To take over a country or territory to make it part of a larger territory

archaeologist A person who digs up and studies artifacts from historic sites

archives A place where historical documents are kept, or a group of documents themselves

artifacts Objects of historical interest made by humans

batteries In military terms, fortified positions for heavy guns

bias Prejudice in favor of or against one thing, person, or group

bombardment Attacked by continuous artillery fire or bombs

cannonade Continuous heavy gunfire

capitulation The act of surrendering

Catholicism The faith, practice, and order of the Roman Catholic Church

cede To give up territory or land

colonize To set up a colony, which is a settlement in one country governed by people from a different country

commemorate To remember and show respect for something

Congress The part of the U.S. government that has the power to make laws

constitution The written laws that govern a territory, state, or nation

context Things that influence and are happening during an event that one needs to know to help historical understanding

convention A formal gathering of people to discuss a special purpose

convert To cause someone to change their religious beliefs

culture The arts, traditions, and other achievements of a society

deportations Official forced movements of people from a country

diligently Showing care in one's work or duties, and the desire to do what's right

diplomat One who acts on a nation's behalf to conduct negotiations with other nations

embellish To add something that is not true to make it more exciting

engraving An art print made from a plate, block, or other surface that has a design cut or carved into it

fictitious Not true; to use the imagination to make things up

fluent To be able to speak and write well in a language

frontier A wilderness area that has not been settled

history Past events and their description

immigrating Moving from one's homeland to another area

independence The fact of being independent from the control of another nation

Indigenous peoples The original peoples of an area

Note: Some **bold-faced** words are defined where they appear in the book.

legendary A famous and well-known story that is passed down from generation to generation

lithograph Printing an image by drawing on a smooth stone with a wax crayon or pencil, rolling black ink over the image, then pressing paper against it to print the image. The image is then colored with paint

Manifest Destiny A term coined that describes the intentions of the United States to expand westward from their original 13 colonies, beginning in the early 1800s

massacre The violent killing of a large number of people

missions Churches or religious centers where religious leaders teach others to convert them to their way of thinking

mythologize To create an exaggerated story from an event and promote it as the truth

negotiations Discussions aimed at reaching an agreement

obstinacy The quality of being stubborn or not able to change or adapt to a situation

outpost A military camp usually located in a remote area

patriotism Strong support and love for one's country

primary sources Firsthand accounts or direct evidence of an event

prospects Chances for future success

republic An independent country or state in which the people elect their government

revoke To cancel or take back

revolution A time of great change; an uprising of the people to overthrow or change government, or gain independence

Roman Catholic A member of the Roman Catholic Church headed by the Pope in Rome

secede To leave an organization or nation

second-class citizens Citizens who do not receive the same rights as other citizens

secondary source Material created by studying primary sources

siege To surround an area, usually with a military force, and cut off supplies and communications coming in or going out

society A group of people living together in an ordered community

source Original document or other piece of evidence; also the origin of artifacts and evidence

sovereignty The authority of a state to govern itself

strategically Planned for a specific purpose, often to block or stop something from happening

translator A person with the ability to understand spoken or written words in one language, and change them to another language

INDEX

Alamo, the,
    Battle of 9, 26–27, 41
    founding of 6–7, 14–15
    The Alamo movies
    Siege of 16–17, 21, 24–27
    10–11, 26
Anglo, definition of 7
Apology Act, the 41
archaeology 13
Austin, Stephen F. 6, 8–9, 18, 22, 32

Béxar 7, 24
Béxar, Siege of 22
bias 20–21
Bonham, James Butler 16, 19, 26
Bowers, Jane 14
Bowie, James 24
broadsides 18–19

Carmel Mission 4–5
Catholicism, Roman 4–5, 6, 8
Cerro Gordo, Battle of 32
Coleto Creek, Battle of 30
context 16, 18
Convention of 1836 30
Cos, General 12, 22
cowboys 7
Creek War 29
Crockett, Davy 8, 28–29

Day, Oriana 4–5
de la Peña, José Enrique 20, 27, 29
Dickinson, Susannah and family 27, 29
Donelson, Andrew Jackson 9

empresarios 7, 8–9, 18

Fannin, James 30

Filisola, Vicente 25
Fisher, George 6

Gadsden Purchase, the 40
Goliad Massacre 30
Gonzales 24, 26
Gonzales, Battle of 22
Guadalupe Hidalgo, Treaty of 33, 34, 36
Guerrero, General 10

historians 4, 10, 16
Houston, Sam 16, 19, 26, 30–31, 32
Huddle, William Henry 33

immigration 9, 41
indigenous peoples 4–5, 6, 29, 37

Joe, Travis's slave 29

Manifest Destiny 18, 37
McArdle, Henry 12, 18, 26–27
Mexican–American War 32–33
Mexican army 9, 22, 24–25, 30, 33, 34–35, 41
Mexican revolutions 8, 41
Mexico 6, 8–9, 22, 32–33, 34, 36–37
Mexico–Texas border 38–39
missions 4–5, 6, 14–15
Morgan, Percy 25

Peña Nieto, President Enrique 40
Polk, President James 33
Potter, Reuben M. 22, 29
primary sources 4, 10, 12, 14, 16, 18–19
Punitive Expedition, the 37, 41

Robinson, Henry R. 12–13
Ruiz, Francisco Antonio 27

San Antonio 6, 8, 22, 29
San Jacinto, Battle of 30–31
Santa Anna, Antonio López de 9, 12, 22, 24, 29, 30, 32–33, 34–35
secondary sources 12–13, 14
Seguín, Juan N. 21, 26
slavery 32, 34, 37
sourcing 16
Spain 8
Spaniards 6–7, 34–35

Tejano, definition of 7
Telegraph and Texas Register 10, 21
Texan army 9, 22, 26
Texan constitution 9
Texas 6–7, 8–9, 40
    Declaration of Independence 26
    Revolution 9, 13, 22
Texian, definition of 7
Tornel y Mendívil, José María 36
Travis, Lieutenant-Colonel William B. 4, 12, 14, 20, 22–23, 24, 27
Trump, President Donald 41

Ukrainian Revolution 38, 40
United States 9, 18, 32–33, 34, 36–37
U.S. Civil War 40

Valesco, Treaty of 31
Villa, Pancho 37, 41

War of 1812, the 8